Chapters

Chapter One

Making a sense of things – Some thoughts on the importance of contentment

This book is about making sense of things; making sense of life – or rather, making sense of my life.

What I will share is certainly not the only way to make sense of things. Everyone has to find a way that suits them. The goal is to understand who you are and why you are here – how you do this is much less important.

The goal for all of us is to become who we are, not just what our parents or friends would like us to be. I believe that we come here to learn a number of lessons. The challenge for all of us is to discover or, perhaps remember, what it is we have come here to learn.

In discovering who we are, and in doing the things we choose to do to learn our lessons, we will find contentment. I say contentment rather than happiness because it is about finding a sense of inner peace, the absence of strife; and thus, our lives will become fulfilled.

To get to this place there is a need to go on one's own journey of self-discovery. People can tell you things – but you need to experience your own lessons. Every person has their own path, their own route to follow. We will share our journey with a number of people who will help us on our way but, ultimately, one has to find and follow one's own path.

My own path is through Spiritualism and, in particular, mediumship.

So, I will share how I came to find this path and aspects of spiritualism.

As I sit and write this, I feel the need to explain why I am doing so.

Perhaps, most importantly, it is to help me to make sense of the things that have happened in my life. Spiritualism has, and still is, helping me to understand who I am and why I am here - although I have a long way to go and so much to learn. If, by reading this, it prompts you to think about your own life then that will be a bonus.

I do believe that becoming who you are and living your life and being true to who you are is very challenging. Making time for yourself to do this is not easy. However, having met a small number of people who are truly content, I know that it is worth all the effort.

By the way, being content, finding your purpose and being 'you' does not stop you experiencing all the issues and problems that life throws up. It can, however, make dealing with them so much easier.

Chapter two

Becoming Me – my journey

My journey began in earnest in 1989. There was an incident that I can still remember vividly. I was bending over cleaning my bath before I got ready for work and I was suddenly struck by an intense feeling of dread. Was this all my life amounted to? Yes, I had a good job with a good pension and my own flat. Materially I was fine, but the dread came from a feeling; if this is all there is then something is missing - something big and very important.

I now feel that I have found what that missing thing is and am working towards making my life whole and complete.

My way is certainly not for everyone. Each person has their own path, their own truth. I do know that when we are ready there will be people around to help us.

My help came through a very special person who I met through my partner, Pat.

In early 1990 Pat and I were going through a difficult patch. It was fortunate that we got back together before we discovered she was diagnosed with cancer. Had the diagnosis happened before, many questions and doubts would have existed between us.

My partner's cancer was called non-Hodgkin's lymphoma, stage 4. The prognosis was poor. She was given about 6 months to live. She opted for a 6-week course of experimental chemotherapy. As well as the chemo she had all kind of complementary therapies; from spiritual healing to colour therapy and joke-telling! She also read a wonderful book by Bernie Seigel; 'Love, Medicine and Miracles'. I would recommend this to anyone dealing with cancer. It is a book about life.

As far as I am aware, all the other people involved with the experimental treatment died within a short period. Pat, however, is still alive, although there were side effects; the main one being damage to her lungs which has been very debilitating for her.

Many people have asked her why she did not die. She would say that in part it was because she fought and had a positive attitude, which may be true. I, however, take a simpler view: It was not her time. She still had things to do; to help others, including me.

Hindsight is wonderful. It can help you to make sense of things in a way that you could not at the time. Just before her cancer diagnosis a medium we know, Jean, rang Pat because a man kept interrupting her when she was performing readings for people. The man said he wanted to speak to a Patsylou. The medium could only think of one person called Pat who this might connect to, hence her call. The conversation went something like this:

Jean: "Do you understand the name Patsylou?"

Pat: "Yes" – (her grandfather called her that – nobody else did)

Jean: "He says that he is the last person you would expect to come through"

Pat – "Yes" (he made fun of spiritualism and even wrote a song to that effect)

Jean – "Do you understand a word that sounds like funts?"

Pat – "Yes – my grandfather would do elephants by moving the sleeve of his smoking jacket like an elephant's trunk. I was only 2 at the time and could only say funts not elephants – but I loved gramps doing this."

Jean- "He's come with a bunch of flowers and wants to say that you will be ok."

After Pat finished her treatment, we went to the Canary Islands for a holiday. Pat's back was playing up and, on her return, we tried a number of things to find a solution for this, but to no avail. Our main worry was that the pain may be an indicator that the cancer had returned.

One Saturday in Brighton, I saw an advert for a psychic/alternative health fayre at Hove Town Hall and thought it would be worth a visit to try to help with Pat's back problem. There was a demonstration of Spiritual Healing just about to start and we went in. They asked for a volunteer and I immediately put up my hand to volunteer Pat. She was given healing by Pauline Swannell. After the session we talked to Pauline who told me that I could do this (healing). Oddly enough the issue for me was not whether I could become a healer but whether I wanted to.

That evening Pat felt so much better and planned to see Pauline at her home the next day. I mulled over what Pauline said that night and by the morning had decided that I would begin training with her to become a Spiritual healer. This meant that I would have to drive from London to Brighton every 2 weeks for 2 years to attend her development sessions.

My first session was interesting and challenging. All the members of the group introduced themselves. Most, if not all, seemed to have lots of experience in the field. I did feel very self-conscious when it came to my turn and I simply said that I was here to learn about healing. However, by the end of the night I knew I was in the right place. Whilst what I was being told was new to me, I felt as if I had always known such things. I knew I had made the right choice.

I did find the sessions challenging. At this time, I was working as a Management Trainer following on from being a teacher and so was used to structure and discipline. Pauline's way of working seemed haphazard, lacking any real structure and she always seemed to go off on a tangent. However, after my 2 years of training and successfully passing my exams to become a healer-member of the National Federation of Spiritual Healers (NFSH) I realised just what a great teacher Pauline was. Pauline never 'told' me anything. She showed me things. She allowed me to find my own path; to find my own truth. When I told Pauline of my revelation, she just laughed and said that she was only a kindergarten teacher!

Pauline was the most spiritual person I have ever met. She is still my role model for teaching and being a spiritualist. She rarely talked about herself and the problems I know that she encountered. She was a person who was just lovely to be with. She was someone who was, what I call, aligned. What she taught is how she lived. A truly magical person.

She said to me once; "When you are ready people will find you. If you need to advertise your wares, then you are not ready".

In 2017 I ran a workshop for a friend on aspects of mediumship and during lunch I had the best compliment I have ever had. A lady said that I reminded her of an old sofa – comfortable to be with. I immediately thought of Pauline and I felt honoured and truly touched.

Since 1992 I have met many wonderful and gifted teachers but none like Pauline, a truly gifted spirit.

My Spiritual development essentially ticked along until I left my job in 2010. I had always belonged to one development group or another, but the main focus was on personal development rather than mediumship. The reality was that work took precedence over any spiritual work. In fact, Pat always said that my real development would, or rather could, only take place when I stopped work.

When I did stop work, rather unexpectedly, I thought at first that I would do more with my spiritual healing. However, spirit had other plans.

I made my first visit to the Arthur Findlay College (AFC) for Psychic Studies (i.e. Mediumship) which was not a great success. I felt like a fish out of water. But I persisted and not long after my first trip to AFC, the church I belonged started running a closed circle for development. Under the guidance of Dorothy Young, I began my development as a Medium. It wasn't planned, it happened.

I attended a number of courses at AFC as part of my ongoing development. My understanding of mediumship and spiritualism began to grow - things began to make sense.

I came to realise that Mediumship is not just about proving that we do not die, thereby helping others to grieve, important though this is. It is also. perhaps more importantly, a way of understanding who you are and what our purpose is - and through that, finding contentment and being at peace with oneself and the world.

The next part is about my understanding of Spiritualism and, in truth, my understanding of life here.

Chapter three

The Guiding Principles (of the Spiritualist National Union)

1. The Fatherhood of God
2. The Brotherhood of Man
3. The Communion of Spirits and the Ministry of Angels
4. The Continuous Existence of the Human Soul.
5. Personal Responsibility
6. Compensation and retribution hereafter for all the good and evil deeds done on earth.
7. Eternal Progress open to every human soul.

Or put more simply:

1. There is a god, a higher being, a higher power.
2. We are all connected.
3. We can talk to those who have 'died'
4. Our spirit or essence continues after the body dies.
5. We are responsible for what we choose to do.

6. We will reap what we sow
7. We come here to learn.

Whilst there may be 7 principles, the one that gets the most airtime is talking to people who have passed to spirit – mediumship. This is both good and bad. Good because it brings people into church and to spiritualism. Bad because often that is all they perceive spiritualism to be – messages from 'dead' relatives. Knowing that we do not die can be the start of trying and choosing what you do, the start of understanding who we are, why we are here and helping us to make sense of our lives and purpose. The trouble is that we have a tendency to take the easy options in life – getting messages is easy, taking responsibility for one's decisions is much harder.

It is not my intention to look at all the principles in order but to rather focus on mediumship and personal responsibility and, in so doing, to touch on all of the principles.

Chapter four

Mediumship

Mediumship is about connecting two worlds; the world of spirit - where we go when our bodies die - and the world where we live now. It is about bringing evidence of people who have died to show that they are still alive (in spirit); to prove that life is eternal, we do not die.

> *If I do not die and I go to the world of spirit when my body dies, then I must have come here for a reason.*

The challenge for all of us is to make sense of this – to understand why we are here. My contention is that mediumship can help us to make sense of life.

So, what does mediumship look like, what's it for and who can do it?

First of all, who can do it? The answer is simple - everybody!

Since we are all spirit it does not seem logical that only some people can connect to the spirit world. You do not have to be 'special' to do this. In fact, I would rather people saw this as ordinary, everyday and normal. There is, however, a caveat. If you feel that you cannot do mediumship then you won't and - as with most things in life - there will be people who are better at it than others. You also have to work at it.

Mediums are not special because they can talk to people who have died.

What is the purpose of mediumship?

1. To show that we do not die – that life is eternal.
2. As a result of 1 to bring healing to the person here – to bring comfort knowing that their loved ones are fine.
3. Help with finding what you are here to do – the purpose of your life.

Mediumship is about providing evidence – information about a 'dead' loved one – information that could only come from that person.

So, what does evidence look like?

When I first became involved with mediumship there was a set way of giving evidence. You were expected to give information such as:

1. Relationship to the sitter (person being read for)
2. How they died
3. Profession
4. Family
5. Hobbies
6. Their house/garden
7. The car they drove
8. Animals/pets.
9. What they looked like – distinguishing features and so on.

The challenge with this approach is that it can sound like someone's CV. It may be factually correct but says little about what the person was like. One needs to make an emotional connection between the sitter and the person in spirit to make it all feel real.

The job of the medium is to represent the person who is in spirit. One needs to animate them, and this cannot be done with facts alone. As a medium, I need to bring in the emotions of the person and I need to remember that I am talking about your mother or husband or sibling and not some kind of energy or vibration. By emotions I mean that I want to share how the person in spirit felt about the sitter, how they showed affection, love. Put simply the medium needs to become the spirit they are representing, and facts alone cannot do this. It is the facts plus the emotion and personality that will make mediumship real.

However, things have changed in the way that mediumship is taught. I became aware of this in 2014 when I was at the Arthur Findlay College.

Put simply, rather than have a series of questions you want answers to be based on the list above, you allow the person in spirit to tell you what the sitter needs. You allow them to tell the story that will make sense. Rather than you try to work out what the person needs or wants, let the spirit do all the hard work. Remembering that one is trying to summarise, for example, a person's life of 70 years into a reading (in a church setting) of about 7 minutes and information that, say, a wife would understand will be different to the information a daughter or friend would understand. The spirit will know exactly what to say to which person. Spirit will tell the story of the person rather than simply give a series of separate facts about the person and so will be that much more coherent.

Put like this it sounds obvious that this is the way for mediums to work. We all know people differently. The challenge for the medium is to let go and not get in the way.

Adopting this approach to mediumship may seem very easy in theory but, like most things, knowing what to do is not the same as actually doing it. Letting go, trusting, working with spirit is challenging, especially if in your day-to-day life you find trust and letting go hard!

The key is to trust your senses – trust what you feel, see, smell. Trusting your feelings is hard, as we spend most of our life being told that thinking is far more important that feeling.

Indeed, we use the word 'emotional' in a derogatory sense much of the time - such as 'she's just being emotional' We are, of course, emotional beings; it is the most natural thing. It is how we react to the world. Emotions are not necessarily good or bad, they simply 'are'. How we react to our emotions is more likely the cause of many of our problems. An incident may cause someone to be angry and frustrated, but one needs to choose carefully how to express this and to whom. It is so true that we often take our anger and frustration out on the people we love the most; the people that often least deserve it.

Mediums receive information in a variety of ways. These are known as 'clairs' (or senses). For me, there are basically four.

Clairvoyance – seeing things

Clairaudience – hearing things

Clairsentience – sensing things – for me, in simple terms it also covers smells and tastes

Claircognisance- you simply know something to be the case

When I first began to work as a medium the hardest thing was to overcome doubt – did I really see that or hear that. I had to learn - and I am still learning - to trust my senses, to trust my feelings. I need to trust my 'gut feeling' – that feeling that comes from my solar plexus, my centre.

Trust in myself is fundamental - not just to mediumship but more importantly to understanding myself and why I am here. I'll return to this later.

The thing to remember for now is that practising mediumship is a good way of building my trust.

There is another aspect to trust; people who come for a reading trust that you will represent their loved ones to the best of your ability. This trust must not be abused. To understand this just go and visit a cemetery – see the headstones and the flowers, read the inscriptions - people are loved and missed.

A keyway of building trust is to say what you sense and see the response. The worst you can be is wrong!

Mediumship is a three-way conversation – the person in spirit, the sitter and the medium. Ideally the medium should have the least to say personally as they are representing the person in spirit. However, in reality the medium has to say what they sense and must endeavour to get that right by not thinking about what the information means.

Using the right language is very important in any reading. We do not all share the same understanding of words. I might describe someone as being a gossip and the sitter might disagree. However, if, for example, I described someone as 'liking to know what was going on' that might be more relevant. If I were to talk about good relationships it would not mean that the people didn't argue often. If you grew up in a family where arguing was common you might see rowing as part and parcel of a good, or normal relationship. In these circumstances the medium always needs to check for understanding.

It's no wonder that relationships are often difficult when we don't always use the same language with the same understanding!

With the clairs I have to say that I do not get too worried about how I receive the information; I don't want to trip over myself with the how… what matters is that I receive the information and share it.

One thing a good teacher told me: As a medium you need to be nosey. If you are shown a briefcase then it is important, and you would need to explore this – what is inside the case? If you are shown a house then you need to explore it – what is the furniture like, is it quiet? The information you share will connect to the sitter and help to bring the person in spirit alive.

If the spirit chooses, they might share something about the sitter's life now. For example: "This week you went to the grave and laid flowers". The purpose of such information is to show that your loved one is still with you; it is not just about memories. You may also be given a message to share with the sitter.

So, mediumship is about 'bringing through' people who have physically died and yet bring healing and hope. Mediumship is not about fortune telling or getting loved one's to make decisions for you.

The key aspect is that as a medium you have to trust what you feel. The more you trust, the better your mediumship and the more aware you will become of yourself.

Why be a medium?

Just because we can do something does not mean that we should do it. It is important for the medium to understand why they want to work with spirit in this way.

If your desire is to help people – there are many ways to do this other than mediumship. Teachers help people, nurses help people, carers help too. There is a worry that if you want to help people you could be simply putting your energy into others and not spending time on your own development. Avoidance!

Are you looking to mediumship to give you fame and fortune?

Is it right to make money from people, often when they are most vulnerable, after the death of a loved one?

What is wrong with getting some recompense for the time you spend with people giving them readings? Is my time not worth something?

There is something to be said for the fact that often, if people get something for free, they do not value it.

I'll come back to this issue later because it is so important. I feel that we need to be self-aware, and understand why we do the things we do because it is about understanding who we are and will help in making sense of the world we live in.

Chapter five

Psychic Readings

In the last chapter I talked about mediumship which is about getting information from people in spirit to prove the continuity of life. A psychic reading is about getting information regarding the sitter's life now.

When I first started to get involved in this area psychic readings were often seen as being somehow inferior to mediumistic readings. There was an expression 'a medium can be a psychic, but a psychic cannot be a medium.' I disagree with this, as everyone can be a medium and also everyone can, if they choose to, be a psychic.

A psychic reading is neither more than, nor less than, a mediumistic reading; it is simply a different reading. It has its place and can be of benefit to a sitter. A psychic reading is essentially a reading about what is going on in the sitter's life. As with mediumistic readings, I believe that we can all do it. A simple way to think about a psychic reading is that it is about using your intuition or 'gut feel'. This is something we do naturally all the time. As always, some are better at it than others.

We all make judgements of people based on feelings. Our 'gut feel' can help us to distinguish between people, those we are drawn to and those we are not. Some people are good at trusting their feelings and some are not. I am not concerned here with the mechanism of intuition. It might be that we remember good decisions and the mind remembers the circumstances. Then if something similar happens, we remember without having to think about it. However, children make decisions based on intuition without having the benefit of the memories adults have. For me, it is enough that I know that intuition works - especially the more I work with it and trust myself.

The challenge is that we are taught to think rather than to feel, so we may have to work at trusting our feelings. We need to be more childlike to work with our emotions and senses.

I feel that a psychic reading begins with intuition, using our emotions and trusting what we feel. However, I also feel that there is a connection to spirit. In the same way, we have to trust what we sense with a mediumistic reading. By this, I mean trust what it feels like in my centre; the same trust applies with a psychic reading. So, all readings, psychic or mediumistic come through the same point, my centre. I accept that there may well be a crossover between the two types of reading, that I may receive information from the spirit world as well as from the person sitting in front of me. Technically the information from spirit is not a mediumistic reading as it may not be evidential in the sense of coming from an identified individual.

So, a good reading is what I call 'intuition plus', but the key part is that I trust what I feel. All information comes through my centre.

What does a good reading look like?

When I teach this, I ask people to look at the sitter and just talk about them. Do they seem happy? Do they seem content or maybe worried? I ask them just to talk about what they sense, what they feel and not to worry. The sitter simply has to say yes, no or don't know. People are always surprised by the amount of information they can perceive. The key is to keep your own mind out of this and just trust what you feel.

I said earlier that it's not just about trusting your intuition; what you see and sense. I will explain why.

I have asked people to face the wall before they do a psychic reading. I have then chosen the sitter. I speak on behalf of the sitter so that the reader has no knowledge of who they are reading for. I then ask the person to do a reading and to begin by sending out their intention to spirit and to expand their aura – feel as if they are expanding their senses into the room. I ask them to trust what they sense and begin. I answer on behalf of the sitter. By asking people to work this way and getting good results it shows that we can get information even when we can receive no audio-visual clues. That is why I call it 'intuition plus'. I have to say that I do not pretend to know how this works, I just know that it does.

Why do people come for psychic readings and what makes it a good reading?

People most often come for a reading because they want help. Something is not right in their life. A reading is not about telling them what to do. A good reading is about helping people to understand what is happening in their life. It is about articulating a feeling that the person has, but cannot make sense of, because it is somehow hidden. When you bring this information out you know that it is right when the individual is somehow not surprised by what is said. The reader is shining a light to open up the darkness and reveal what is hidden. As always it is about things 'feeling right'.

A good reading will help the person find their own resolution.

Can you tell the future?

In general, the answer is no as we all have free will. I could say to a sitter that a new job is on the horizon but if the person does not actually apply for a job it is very unlikely that my prediction will come true. However, I have met people who have shared future insights that have come to fruition. Indeed, this has happened to me.

Some twelve years ago, out of the blue, I was told by my Human Resources Director at my workplace that my role would no longer exist. I needed to think about my future. I was given three weeks to think about what I wanted to help me leave the business. At the time the standard redundancy package was twelve months pay; not enough for me to stop work and I was too young to take my pension. To say that I was shocked, surprised and angry would be an understatement. My partner's view was unequivocal, this would be the best thing to happen; to leave the business, stop commuting and give me the time to work on my spiritual development. I was not convinced. I went to see a good medium; someone I had known for over 20 years, for a reading. From that reading came two things that I still recall today. Firstly, he said that the easy option would be to try and stay with the company (this was not compulsory redundancy) or the hard, and better, option would be to leave and develop myself. Secondly, he said that there would be more money available.

As a result of this conversation I spoke to a number of people in Human Resources to see how I might negotiate for more money. One of the things that came up was to look at some kind of pro rata bonus which might bring in another 1-2 months of pay. I realised that there was no point in being angry with the Director about what was happening. I knew that she could easily put up with a 10-minute rant and I would get nothing.

At the end of three weeks I went to the meeting with the Director. When she asked what I wanted I surprised myself by saying that I did not feel that I could negotiate with her. I had seen her negotiate with others and knew this was not a level playing field by any stretch of the imagination. She sat and thought for a few moments and shared her thoughts about what to give me. The bottom line was that she offered me an extra 6 months' pay – much more than I had possibly expected. I am not sure that this would have been the outcome had I not put a lot of energy and thought into what the medium said. Looking back, it was the best decision I made. Both the medium and my partner were right!

So, can we see into the future? I do believe that some people can offer insights, but free will can impact on whether things will come to pass.

If a medium does have the ability to see into the future it may be because they are spending too much time looking at the future with the danger that they spend much less time living in the present. I do not believe that this is a good thing for them. We learn and grow because of what we do now.

Can cards be used in psychic readings?

The simple answer is yes. Mediums often use cards, such as oracle cards or angel cards or tarot cards.

The sitter shuffles the pack of cards and chooses the card or cards to be used. The reading is based on the content of the cards and what it suggests to the reader.

When I ran a development circle in Canada, I asked people to pair up and do a psychic reading in order to build their trust and confidence. I had a pack of cards and asked people to choose one. I explained that it would help with the reading. I walked around the room encouraging and helping as necessary while people worked. I sat with one pair who were experiencing difficulties. The reader said that they could get nothing from the card. I asked her to put the card down for the moment and then asked her to look at the sitter and to simply tell me what came to her. She began: 'There is a problem with a relationship', I asked her who the problem was with. She said it was with her husband. Then she stopped herself after the sitter said yes adding that she knew the sitter as a friend and was not aware of this problem. I then asked the reader to look at the card that she had chosen. It was the marriage card!

The more I work with psychic readings, the more I like them; especially as a tool for teaching. It is a great way to build confidence and trust. As always, the more we trust, the more information we are given from such readings.

The key is to say what you feel. Not to let thinking obstruct your senses. Trust what feels right at your centre. Simplicity is the key here. Humans do have a tendency to overcomplicate things. There is also the danger of dismissing things that we do not fully understand.

It is easy to say 'let go and trust yourself' but it can be harder to actually do in practise. There is truth in the statement that; 'If I think I can't do something then I will not be able to do it. If I think I can do something, then there is a good chance that I will be able to do it.'

Chapter six

Spiritual Healing

Sometimes called the highest form of mediumship.

Defined by the Spiritualist National Union (SNU) as: "A form of healing by the use of forces and energies from the world of spirit, channelled through the healer by the laying on of hands on or near the body, or prayer, or the direction of thought from a distance."

It is the most obvious example of letting go and letting God take over

For me, Reiki, crystal healing, colour healing, spiritual healing and any other forms of healing all come from the same place: Spirit, God – call it what you like but remember it is not from us. It comes from a higher power.

It is interesting that when I was taught to become a spiritual healer I was never taught to heal. The reason is obvious now. I am not the one doing the healing! I am simply allowing myself to be a channel for spirit to work through me. That seems very simple but why, then, does it take two years of training if you are not actually doing the work?

I realise that it is about one's development, understanding who you are and why you are doing this. If you think that healing is just about helping others, then you are liable to get into difficulties.

On my second training weekend I came across what I called the 'dead dog syndrome'. A number of people seemed to break down, be in tears and felt unable to continue on the course. I found it all a bit strange as the course did not seem particularly challenging or personal to me. I talked to a number of people and the reason for the problem seemed to stem from the fact that some people had chosen to work as healers to help others but had neglected their own personal development. They had forgotten to help themselves first.

Putting yourself first is often an area that causes confusion for people. Some people imagine that if you put yourself first you are being selfish and as such are behaving badly. For me, I see that putting yourself first is a necessity. How can I help others if I am not fit and well in the first place? I differentiate between being selfish and being self-centred. Self-centred means "me, me, me" it's all about me and what I want. Being self-centred links to narcissism, being unable to accept criticism, more worried about looking good than doing good.

One of the challenges we face in this space is that, in general, we are taught facts about the world or facts about the things that are around us but spend little or no time trying to understand who we are. We don't talk easily about our emotions, our feelings. We separate the head and the heart rather than see them as part of a whole person. Our society would appear to value thinking above feelings. I do believe that thinking is as important as feeling and that integration is better than separation

Two years training to be a healer does seem like a long time to understand that it's not you that does the healing. In order to let go and let spirit come through, you do need to understand who you are.

You also need to understand the Code of Conduct to ensure that you behave properly and professionally.

Behaving professionally is obviously important. Spiritual Healing is a complementary therapy, it works in harmony with traditional medicine. There can be no promises of cures. People who come for healing are often vulnerable and are seeing you as a last resort; having exhausted all other therapies. Their trust must not be abused. Sadly, I have heard many horror stories of 'healers' telling people to stop their chemotherapy and take vitamins. Such people do a grave disservice to the people they purport to heal. Healers cannot and must not diagnose – that is for Doctors alone.

Some questions and answers to help explain what spiritual healing is.

Do you need to believe in Spiritual Healing for it to work? (Is it faith Healing?)

The simple answer is no. However, if you think it won't work, this may well affect the outcome. Why have healing if you are against it?

For the healer it is about letting go and letting spirit do what is needed for the person.

Can you guarantee an outcome – a cure?

Quite simply NO. However, it is important to remember that healing is nonnegative – done properly, it can do no harm.

Do you need to touch?

No. You can work close to the body. You can actually touch the body appropriately (for example, the shoulders) or you can work where the person can be some distance from the healer. Touch can be important for some people and can provide comfort.

Where does the healing come from?

The Healing comes from God. It seems strange as I write the word 'God'. I accept it to be true but recognise that this word does put a lot of people off. Some people are more comfortable with expressions such as Spirit, or Universal Energy. The key point is that the healing comes through us and not from us. We are simply the channel that the healing passes through. You have to be true to yourself and for me I am happy with God.

Does Healing work?

Yes, it can - see cases below. It can have a physical impact and help remedy a problem. Sometimes it may simply allow people a bit of breathing space to take stock of their lives and help them to make changes that are needed. A common event after a healing session is for the person to sleep well, often for the first time in ages. A good night's sleep can have a huge impact on well-being.

The healing may be about helping people to come to terms with the end of their life. It is not always about making people better.

Healing is also about telling people that they have a role in their health too! For example, if a person comes for healing about a bad back and they spend all day digging in the garden – then, if they continue digging after healing, their back may still be a problem. Sometimes people need to change aspects of their life. People always have a choice about what they do, even if the choices are not always easy. If gardening is your living, giving it up may not be possible.

I have seen healing make a difference and I know that it works. However, one of the challenges is about feedback, or rather, the lack of. We all like to get feedback on what we do, especially the positive kind. It makes us feel good, feel valued. Often though, people will come for a healing session and not come back again and so we don't know what the outcome of the healing was which can be slightly frustrating. Sometimes the feedback can make you smile. I remember one case when I asked the person how they felt after the first session. They said that they had felt nothing. When I asked how they had slept after the session, they said they had slept really well for the first time in ages! I decided not to ask why they had come back for more healing.

How does Healing work?

I have heard a number of people talk about energy and vibrations and how this brings about healing. I have to say I do not hold with this. I prefer to adopt the stance that Harry Edwards (a famous healer) took – that he did not need to know how healing works that it is enough to know that it does.

If you have never tried Spiritual Healing, I would encourage you to try it. Most Spiritualist

Churches offer healing in exchange for a donation.

An important aspect of healing that connects to Spiritualism is personal responsibility. Healing can bring great benefit, but we bear some responsibility for our lifestyle that contributes to our well-being.

Case 1: Philip

Philip was suffering from a blood cancer and was having regular chemotherapy. He came for healing regularly until he passed. We always talked a lot during our sessions, and he told me that he enjoyed our time together. Philip gave me a lovely compliment when he recalled having a difficult chemotherapy session and he said he could hear me telling him to just get on with it, which helped him to get through the session. Towards the end of his life he talked a lot about his relationships with his wife and family. I realised that these conversations were not meant for me and I encouraged him to share these thoughts and feelings with his family.

Philip helped me to understand that healing is about helping people, it's not always about getting better.

Case 2: Mark

As a result of the work I was doing with Philip, a lady asked if I would see her father who was having treatment for cancer. Of course, I agreed to.

Whilst I knew that Mark had cancer I did not know until the first meeting that he had already lost an arm and most of his shoulder to the disease. At the first, and only session I asked him what he wanted, explaining that I didn't think there was much I could do about the missing arm. The tension was released through laughter. It's interesting how humour can help in the most difficult of situations. I gave healing and trusted that he would get what he needed, if not what he wanted. There was a sadness with this case as the person who asked me to see Mark never spoke to me again. I think that she was hoping for a miracle that never came.

It's as if death is the elephant in the room. People generally do not like to talk about death which is sad in many ways. It will happen to us all and I believe that if we work with this knowledge it can help us to make more of our lives. It was clear from my conversation with Mark that he was aware that his time was limited and that there were still things to be done.

Case 3: Mary

Mary came to see me and told me that she was suffering from a brain tumour. I took her through a meditation followed by a healing session. She did not talk very much during the session, which is not unusual. Mary never came back. Sometime later I heard from a mutual acquaintance that just after she saw me, she went back to the hospital for a scan and they told her the tumour had reduced. Apparently, this scared her so much that she felt she could not come back to see me.

Case 4: Andrew

I must declare an interest here as Andrew was and still is a very good friend of mine. We were away travelling in Vietnam and Andrew had been complaining about a bad back. I offered to do some healing and he accepted. During the healing Andrew heard and felt his back click back into place. It is important to note that when I do a healing session, I work close to, but do not touch, the body of the person.

Andrew has never had a problem with his back again.

Case 5: Pat

I should declare an interest here as Pat is my partner.

We were out walking one afternoon in autumn and Pat damaged her ankle by walking into a hole in the pavement that was covered in leaves. As soon as we got to my flat, I asked her to sit on the sofa and I placed my hands around her ankle. Pat described the sensation as having the small hands of children manipulating her ankle. She said it was a very pleasant sensation. She travelled home to Brighton the next day. Her ankle was troubling her, so she found herself 2 days later having her ankle x rayed. The Consultant asked her when she had the accident as the ankle did have a fracture, when told it was 4 days earlier, he expressed surprise, as it looked as it had happened several weeks ago due to the healing on the fracture.

One of the important aspects of healing is that it has helped me to learn and to grow. It has helped me to trust, to let go and let God. To recognise and accept my emotions and intuition, to trust my judgement. I have become much more aware of who I am and to believe in who I am. I have also learned to combine my intuition with my logical mind.

The challenge for me, and for all of us, is how to use this information to discover what it is we choose to do with our lives.

Chapter seven

Doing the Right Thing

I have become more aware of myself and have learnt to trust my gut feel - my intuition - and so how do I use this new information for my development, for my life?

I believe that we are here on Earth for a reason, that we have lessons to learn before we go back. Even if you don't subscribe to the Spiritualist agenda there is still the question of how to make the most of our lives. How do we find contentment?

What's next? This is the hard part, many of us are looking for a simple step process to follow, some kind of simple solution that does not require too much effort on our part. Sadly, I do not believe this to be possible, and that is as it should be. To embark on a journey or quest about your life is so important and significant that it would only be reasonable to expect to commit a significant amount of energy and resources to it. Surely putting time and energy into this is not too much to ask especially given the outcome you are looking for – contentment!

Contentment, and I choose the word carefully, means being at peace with yourself and those around you. It is not a fixed space, but rather a state of being. To be in this state no matter what happens to you - whatever life throws at you - you are in the right place to deal with things. Contentment is not happiness. Happiness comes and goes. Contentment, or being at peace, just feels right. It is an honourable aim. It will be unique to each person. How will you know when you are there? It's simple – it will feel right. And having worked on trusting yourself, you will know.

So, how do I go from understanding 'me', to finding what to do?

The Seven Principles of Spiritualism provide a framework.

We are all connected and so it is reasonable to treat people with kindness and respect. I am responsible for what I do and so I choose what I do. If I behave badly then I am accountable and will have to answer for my behaviour at some time. I can learn from all the things I do.

However, it does not provide specific guidance on what we can choose to do.

The Gospel of the Redman[1] is slightly more specific:

1. There is one great Spirit, the creator and ruler of all things, to whom we are responsible.

2. Having arrived on this earth, the first duty of man (or woman) is the attainment of perfect manhood, which is the just development of every part and power that go to make a man. He must achieve manhood in the body way, mind way, spirit way and the service way. (Be the best you can with all of your gifts)

3. Having attained the high manhood, he must consecrate that manhood to the service of his people.

---

[1] Gospel of the Redman - Ernest Thompson Seaton and Julia Seaton 2005 World Wisdom Books.

4. The soul of man is immortal. Where it came from or where it goes, he does not know. But when his time comes to die, he should remember that he is going to the next world. What the next life contains for him, he has no means of ascertaining. Nevertheless, he should not approach it with fear and trembling, repenting and weeping over such things as he has left undone, or such things as he should not have done. He should rest assured that he has done the best with the gifts and limitations that were his, and that his condition there will be governed by his record and behaviour here. Therefore, let him sing his death song, and go out like a hero going home.

This, to me, just seems to be common sense. Make the most of the gifts that you have and use them to be of service to others. If you do this you will reach the end of life with few, if any, regrets because you will have led a full and complete life.

It's important to spend time on yourself, understanding who you are and then you have to use your gifts to help others. It is about my own journey, finding out why I am here and what lessons I have to learn and part of that is also about others (the Brotherhood of Man – we are all connected).

There is nothing new about the importance of service. Kahlil Gibran[2] wrote about this early in the last century:

> *"A little knowledge that acts is worth infinitely more than knowledge that is idle. If your knowledge teaches you not the value of things, and frees you not from the bondage to matter, you shall never come near the throne of truth. If your knowledge teaches you not to rise above human weakness and misery and lead your fellow man on the right path, you are indeed a man of little worth and will remain such until judgement day."*

---

[2] A Second Treasury of Kahlil Gibran translated by Anthony Ferris. Mandarin Paperbacks 1992

We do become less when we do not share. I do not lose something when I share my knowledge and understanding rather, I add to others by doing so.

So, I've spent time understanding who I am and recognising that I am able to trust my feelings and judgement. The next stage is to do those things that are right for me, to live a life that is in harmony and bring me to experience a true sense of contentment.

Chapter eight

Before we begin to look at what we can do, some thoughts…

You can't help people who aren't ready to be helped; until they are ready nothing will happen. I can, and will, suggest things to help but until someone is ready, I could be whistling in the wind for all the good it may do.

You have to accept who you are before you can begin. I have to work with my gifts, my strengths and not those of others. This may sound obvious. You may not be surprised by the fact that many people beat themselves up because they do not feel that they have sorted out their life at their age.

Accept that now is the time to start, if you are ready. Saying that you will be ready to start when the children are grown up, when the mortgage is paid off, when you retire (delete as appropriate), generally means that you may never get around to doing something. You can always find a reason **not** to do something. Yes, we do need to manage our responsibilities but that does not necessarily mean that we can't do something. Be aware and conscious of the decisions that you choose to take – or not.

Acceptance is about you, not what you do. We are all individual and unique. I do not need to do anything to make me unique – I simply am. I might want to be a great high jumper, but for me, at 5 feet nothing my optimism may not be enough to lift me over a 6-foot bar!

Ahh! I hear you cry. Why are you limiting yourself? There is a fine line between thinking you can do anything and the fact that we do have physical and mental limitations. Stretch yourself and go for things. However, you are far more likely to be successful when you understand and play to your strengths. I may not be able to jump over 6 feet, but I can jump the highest I can.

I have a personal wariness of repeating mantras such as "I want to be rich/I will be rich/I deserve to be rich" and assuming that on their own this will be enough to secure your desire.

By all means be positive but it is important to turn such thoughts into action and, through that action, move towards achieving your goal.

A wish without a plan is just that, a wish.

Your starting point is always where you are, not where you might want to be.

The importance of being 'you' cannot be overstated.

Where I worked in the 1990s there was a redundancy programme and a number of colleagues took advantage of the opportunity to use the money to make positive life changes. Michael decided that he would retrain as a Counsellor, something that he had always wanted to do. Before starting his training, he decided to use some of the redundancy money to fund a trip to India and then do some further travelling. A good friend of his, Phillip, was also taken by the idea of travel and thought they might travel together. Phillip's boss, who knew him well, cautioned against such a drastic move and said that if he really wanted to travel then he would give him time off to see if it would be better for him rather than take the redundancy package and have no way back. Phillip decided to ignore the offer of help, took the package and left the company. He flew to India, spent a day there and then realised that this was not for him. His redundancy money did not last for very long and he spent a long time trying to return to full-time employment.

Be you and not someone else. Sometimes we are better off taking small steps when we want to change things.

Change the way you look at things

Contentment is not a fixed place. Your life is not suddenly over when you find contentment. All your struggles do not cease. Rather, it means that you are at peace and able to deal with what challenges life will throw at you. You are ready to continue to grow through the lessons you will continue to be given. Indeed, I would go so far as to say that finding contentment is perhaps the start point of learning the things you have come here to learn.

Letting Go – we can't hold on to everything

As we take on new things, try them and see if they work. Be prepared to let things go.

I think of this as travelling with a backpack, As I gather more experiences, the pack gets bigger. However, there is a limit to how much I can carry. If I want to take on new things, I have to let some things go. I can still carry the learning from the things I have done, but I do not need to carry the whole experience.

There is also the point that as I take on new experiences some of my old views may not be compatible. I have a choice: I can either grow or remain stuck in the past. I choose to grow.

Some of my friends will be fine with the new things that I do, and some will not. This is not necessarily a problem as long as they allow you to do the new stuff without knocking you back all the time.

This is an important issue. It took me some time to come to terms with it. Why should your friends agree with all that you do? Why should your friends be interested in all the things that you do? Friendship is, in part, about accepting people for who they are, warts and all. We do not need to be a clone to be a friend.

All this comes back to the idea that people we know may not always be with us, people come in to and out of our lives. Rather than see this as some kind of failure, accept it as the natural order of things. Indeed, how many relationships turn very sour because people feel they should stay together even though they have grown apart. How much better it would be for all parties, if people accepted the situation and parted with good grace. Rather enjoy the time we spend together and, if it is time to part, trust your feelings and let go with kindness.

There is a poem by an unknown author that talks about meeting people:

> *People come into your life for a reason, a season or a lifetime. When you figure out which one it is you will know what to do for each person*
>
> *…*
>
> *Lifetime relationships teach lifetime lessons, things you must build upon in order to have a solid emotional foundation. Your job is to accept the lesson, love the person and put what you have learnt to use in all other relationships and areas of your life. It is said that love is blind, but friendship is clairvoyant.*

The sentiment is important. People come into our lives and help us and not everyone needs to be with us for the long haul. Be thankful for those who come to help and don't forget that we have roles to play in the lives of others too. Remember to be kind as it will have a positive impact on those that you come across and will make a difference.

I do believe that if you love someone then you will let them go if that is what they want because you want what they want.

As you begin to work on yourself there will be some people who stay and support you, and there will be some that you leave behind.

Relationships are always two way. If you <u>both</u> want things to work, then there is a greater likelihood that they will. However, if one person doesn't, then the relationship is finished, whether you like it or not.

It is also about choice. Choose to be with positive people. Leave the complainers, the negative one's behind. It is always amazing how much you can do when you are surrounded by positive and encouraging people.

Reality checks from friends are always to be encouraged, but not too much cynicism or cockeyed optimism.

Language

Change your language, change your thoughts, change the outcome

Language is powerful and important, especially when we look at change. Changing words changes how we see things.

For example, words such as 'should' are essentially guilt words as in, 'I should have gone to see my mother – I feel guilty about not seeing her'. Much better to say that 'I have chosen to see my mother', or more likely, 'I have chosen not to see my mother, as I have other more pressing matters at the moment'.

When people say; 'I don't have a choice about……' What they are really saying is that there may be a choice, but it is difficult, and I will more than likely upset someone, which I don't want to do, and so I regard what is happening as giving me no choice.

Responsibility and choice go hand in glove. I am responsible for the choices that I make. Choices have consequences, some are not important, but some are. Not everyone will like the choices that I make.

I have to say that, as you become who you are, there is a need to understand and accept this.

Another example; 'I'll try to do this……' It's like having permission to fail before you begin. A better expression is; 'I will do…….'

Think about what you are saying, are you empowering yourself or giving your power away? It's not just about the use of positive words, it is about choice and responsibility. It is ok not to do something… but be honest.

It reminds me of the Spiritualist Principle of Personal Responsibility, I am not responsible for all the things that happen to me, but I am responsible for how I respond to these things.

I am reminded of the idea that thought precedes action. If you think you will fail then, more than likely, you will. If you think you can succeed, then you have at least given yourself a fighting chance.

Jens Voigt, a famous tour de France cyclist was asked if he would go for a stage win even if he only had a 10% chance of victory. "Yes", he answered. A 10% chance was much better than no chance!

I have met cancer sufferers who when told that their illness gave them only a 15% chance of survival, were the people who took the view that they would be part of the 15%. Give yourself that chance in whatever you choose to do, to be successful.

Chapter nine

Contentment

It's about you, not everyone else.

This is all about finding out understanding who you are, why you are here and spending your time doing what you are supposed to be doing. It is my belief that if we do what we are supposed to do then we will find contentment. For contentment also read being at peace.

Your move to finding contentment is about you. It is not about a comparison with others.

We spend a lot of our time comparing ourselves to others. Studies of well-being and wealth show that our sense of well-being is influenced significantly by the way we compare ourselves to friends and neighbours, rather than some stand-alone measure.

We seem to gain some perverse pleasure from comparisons.

> *'If my life is not great, I can somehow feel better because my neighbour is worse off.'*

It is an illusion. It's as if we are both drowning, but because my neighbour is drowning faster, I don't feel as bad. However, I am still drowning! Comparisons take me away from my problem, but they don't actually help me solve my problem.

Contentment is about me. I wish it for all.

Importantly, I do not need to reference anyone else. Either I am contented, or I am not. I may care about friends and family but, unless I can take action personally to change their circumstances, my contentment does not depend on them.

I may offer help and support to others, but I am not here to live their lives for them. I am not here to take on their problems. It's like the oxygen masks that come down in aircraft when there are problems: You put your mask on first before helping others.

This is not about ignoring the Spiritualist principle of the Brotherhood of Man. It is important to help others where and when you can, but it is not always about doing things for them. We all have lessons to learn and we have to do them on our own. Sometimes letting people fail may look as if we are uncaring but it might be the best way for the person to learn lessons. Sometimes the best support we can give is to simply be there.

Making comparisons between yourself and others, who may seem to have progressed more than you, are also not helpful. We all have lessons to learn and they may be different lessons for each of us. Also, there will be things we find easy to do and some things that are hard and those, again, will be different for all of us.

Perhaps, more importantly, looking at the progress or otherwise of others takes you away from yourself. Rather than compare yourself to others, why not ask and learn from the experience of others. Finding contentment is not a competition.

Chapter ten

A Review of where we are

We have looked at mediumship from the point of view of helping you to understand who you are, to get used to listening to and trusting yourself.

Mediumship is not the only way to get to this point.

From this point of becoming 'me' you are now in a position to find out what you could choose to do to bring contentment to your life.

Contentment comes from being me and doing those things that are right for me. Contentment is also connected to the notion that I have come here for a reason and there are lessons for me to learn and when I work towards these reasons, I know that I am doing the right things.

We each have our own path to follow – people are there to guide and help us, but they cannot do things for us. There are many fellow travellers, but their paths are not exactly the same as ours.

Chapter eleven

Things that can help

We now turn to look at what things we could do to help us on our journey.

I want to share a quote from Khalil Gibran[3] in the Prophet – when he talks about teaching:

> *"No man can teach you aught but that which already lies half asleep in the dawning of your knowledge……. (the teacher) if he is indeed wise he does not bid you enter the house of his wisdom, but rather leads you to the threshold of you own mind……..the astronomer may speak to you of his understanding of space, but he cannot give you his understanding."*

Teachers cannot tell us what path we have to follow but they can inspire us to take the first

---

[3] The Prophet, Kahlil Gibran. Mandarin Paperback 1992.

steps on our own journey of self-discovery and the magic that that contains.

I will share some things that I believe will help you on your way.

"Being busy is overrated if you ask me" – Printed on a label attached to a Winnie the Pooh bear I was given.

Being busy is something that can be all too familiar to us whether it is at work, home or, more often, both. There's an old saying that if you want something done then ask a busy person.

The question that is rarely asked though, is being busy the same as doing the right thing?

Presenteeism, or being at work for long hours, is often seen as a badge of honour. The question though is, are we paid for the hours we work (some people are) or are we paid for the value we bring to work? If you are very busy, where is the time to reflect, to take stock? I have to say that I would rather pay people for their value-add to a business rather than simply for the hours they put in.

If we are busy it can be easy to feel as if we are on a treadmill where we have to keep going. Getting off never seems like an option.

Being busy helps you to be lazy, you have an excuse not to make time for you. Being busy is easy, it's what most people do. Taking, or making time for yourself is hard. The questions to ask and the answers may appear difficult mainly because, I suspect, we aren't used to thinking about ourselves.

Culturally we have problems with not being busy. If you are seen at work being inactive, for example thinking, you are more likely to be thought idle. Letting people work from home can be challenging too, people are not always trusted just to get on with things.

Our lives are often busy, which is normal and ok. However, it is not ok if we always seem to be busy. If you want to find out if what you are doing is right for you, you are unlikely to make progress if you make no time for yourself.

Being busy places greater value on doing things rather than being. It's like quantity over quality. Yes, we are here to learn things, so we need to do things, but we need to ensure that we are doing the right things.

Choose to make time for yourself.

"What is this life if, full of care, we have no time to stand and stare"

W. H. Davies [4]

If we are not careful, we will stay on a treadmill, head down, being busy, feeling tired and then suddenly we will stop and wonder where our life went. We have been so busy that we have forgotten that we are on a journey of sorts and have forgotten to enjoy the ride. To continue the analogy, it's like getting on a train and forgetting to get off at the stops en-route so that we enjoy the journey. Our lives are also about our journey, not just arriving at the destination.

This makes me think of time wasters. Have you ever been totally absorbed or transfixed by something so that you simply forgot about time and wonder where the hours went? I have, many times. I have to say that I gained great pleasure from watching my kittens when we bred Cornish rex cats. It was just wonderful to watch the kittens play. I remember a time when I decided it was time to bring the kittens from

[4] William Henry Davies – Leisure. The Nations Poems BBC.

the upstairs to the kitchen. Having carried all five kittens down, Topsy, their mother, decided that was not right. She made a kind of chirruping sound and the kittens followed her back upstairs. It was quite magical to watch and put me in my place!

It took me sometime to realise that watching the kittens was not time wasting, it was teaching me to enjoy the real pleasures of life.

The same applies to relationships, it's not always about what the two of you do together. It's easy to undervalue or underestimate the importance of just being together. I love just being with my partner even if we are in different rooms in the house.

Life is about enjoying the everyday, the mundane and the humdrum.

It is often in the quiet, sitting alone, that we can begin to see and enjoy our lives.

Make time to stand and stare!

Our time here is limited we owe it to ourselves to make the most of our lives by doing the right things, being ourselves and giving ourselves the time to do it.

Meditation

Meditation takes many forms. From guided walks to the chanting of mantras. There is also the simplicity of sitting quietly. The importance of meditation comes from making time for oneself. It means that I am important, and I will make time for myself.

Meditation is about 'me'. It doesn't matter what practise you follow. Find the one or many that suit you. For me, it is important that the practise helps me to understand who I am.

It is about letting go and allowing yourself to be. You are not looking for an outcome. It is about trust.

You can ask for help. I will often get an answer when I am washing the dishes or, more likely for me, when I am off cycling. I am often surprised by what pops into my head as I slowly climb a hill. I am always grateful for the help I get.

Remember to always find what suits you.

Make time for yourself.

Chapter twelve

Death

It is hard to understate the importance of death. It is the scariest thing for most of us. I wonder if the fear is connected to the loss of self. The idea that when we die what is 'me' is somehow lost.

What is clear is that it is a taboo subject. You only have to listen to the way we talk in the media about how we are beating cancer, that fewer people are dying from heart disease and so forth. What is not made clear is that all of us will die. Our physical bodies will decompose, and we will no longer be here in our current form.

We shy away from talking about death. I have met a number of people who will not write a will for fear that it will jinx their lives and somehow bring on their death!

If we live in the fear of death there is the danger that we stop living, stop making the most of ourselves, stop being ourselves and that would be a waste. We would hide ourselves away and forget the joy that life can bring.

As Tennyson[5] said; "It is better to have loved and lost, than never to have loved at all" – just change the word 'loved' to 'lived'!

Death provides a marker for our lives. Irrespective of what you believe will happen to us after death our lives here in our current form will come to an end.

We can use this information to inform our lives positively. How much better to live your life truthfully so that when you get to the end of your life you can feel that you have made the most of your life and have few, if any, regrets.

This is not about making perfect decisions, but it is about always making the best decision at the time, being true to yourself and doing the best you can. We will all make mistakes. The key is to learn from them and not repeat them.

Death leaves me in no doubt that my time here is limited. I can choose to use this knowledge

---

[5] Alfred Lord Tennyson – In Memoriam.

to make the most of my time; to drive me to find contentment.

There was a lovely programme on television recently which talked about death. One of the things that stayed in my mind was a comment from a Professor, in charge of a hospice, who said that a large part of his role was to help people come to terms with the end of their life. What struck me was that this was the kind of thing that should be shared with people well before the end so that they could do more with their lives. They could make positive changes to help them come to terms with their life and death.

I find this interesting because it makes me think about my own beliefs, about my life after death. What stands out for me is that a belief in the afterlife does not let me forget about my life. Rather the reverse. I have come here for a reason and it is important that I live my life fully so that I learn those things I need to.

Just as we are not taught about death, we are not taught about grief; the importance of the grieving process and helping us to come to terms with loss. In Britain we generally do not go in for public expressions of grief – Princess Diana's death notwithstanding. We seem to prefer the idea of the stiff upper lip. We tend to look with disdain at those cultures where people sob and scream at funerals. I wonder if we simply struggle to understand how much those expressions are very positive in helping people come to terms with death?

Emotional constipation is not healthy. Emotions are meant to be expressed so we let them pass through us. They help us to deal with life.

I would encourage you to think about death and to find your way to make some sense of it, to embrace it rather than be paralysed by fear.

I once did a meditation on death. The image that stayed with me was of me walking with two suitcases and that when I died, I simply let go of the suitcases. I let go of my life and all the things in it. It made me think that I should not believe that all the things I have are important, some are, but most are really not so important.

Be careful what you cling to. Material things are of little consequence. The one thing that I want to share is that this experience was not frightening.

This leads me on to one group that does not fear death, people who have had a near death experience. A common theme appears to be the sense of travelling along a tunnel, being drawn to a light and an incredible sense of peace and love. A love that transcends anything experienced on earth. The individuals seem to be told that it is not their time and, often reluctantly, they come back. It's as if they approach their transition from here to there with no fear, more a sense of going home to be with their loved ones.

Chapter thirteen

God

The idea of God is a challenging one, even in Spiritualism. If you go to a Spiritualist service you are likely to come away with the idea that it is all about mediumship rather than something that is above us all, that we are a part of something much bigger. I feel that people love the mediumship and the messages of hope and love but are generally less keen on the lessons and the learning. People are often drawn to the Spiritualist Church because of the messages and the sense of magic that is connected to this. Talk of God seems to take them back to the churches that they have left. They like the personal aspects of spiritualism but talk of God makes it all seem impersonal. People are also drawn to crystals, tarot cards, angels, things that are essentially not seen as part of our everyday lives. There is a belief that there is something more, but many seem uncomfortable with the notion of God, or a God.

For me, everything comes under God. I have the sense that my purpose in life is ultimately about accepting that I am part of God. I accept that the notion of God is problematic for many people. The Judeo-Christian notion of a God who is some kind of person (man-like) glorified as a king on a throne sits uncomfortably with many.

I have met mediums who are happy to give messages from loved one's who have died but have difficulties with the idea of God.

Churches - both Christian and Spiritualist - are closing and yet there is growing interest in things like angels and spiritual healing – things that are plainly not part of this world.

Does God need a makeover, a new PR team to promote him/her/it, positively? I think not, but I do feel that we need to find a way of understanding what God means to us, a universal spirit, something big, unconditional love. I do believe that there is something more than us, important though we like to think of ourselves. Maybe we are not the centre of the universe!

I am uncomfortable with religious fundamentalism of any kind. It is easy to see how they have grown with their seductive talk of 'just do as we say, and heaven awaits'. 'Only those who follow our rules will be saved, hell and damnation await all others'. This does not sit well with me or my belief in personal responsibility and lifelong learning. I also cannot forget the importance of the Brotherhood of Man; we are all connected. Why seek to divide something that cannot be divided?

I do not believe it matters which religion you believe in. There are many paths to God. Spiritualism certainly does not have a monopoly on access to God. It would be both arrogant and wrong for anyone to believe this.

What matters is not your choice of religion, but rather your kindness.

Kindness matters. It can help people and makes a difference. I am just beginning to understand how important this is. Kindness is open to all; you don't need money or education to show it. Whether you have given a kindness or received it you know that it feels right – that's all there is to it.

I do not recognise a God that is not tolerant, loving and kind. I do recognise people who, sadly are like that.

Go with the Flow…

There is a lovely poem by Rumi[6] The Guest House.

> *"This being human is a guest house,*
>
> *Every morning a new arrival.*
>
> *A joy, a depression, a meanness,*
>
> *Some momentary awareness comes*
>
> *As an unexpected visitor.*
>
> *Welcome and entertain them all!*
>
> *……...*
>
> *Be grateful for whoever comes,*
>
> *Because each has been sent*
>
> *As a guide from beyond."*

Personal responsibility is an important aspect of spiritualism. However, it does not mean that we can control all of the things that happen to us. Things happen to us that we would not choose. We lose jobs, divorce, become ill. Whilst I may not choose these things, I can

---

[6] Rumi – The Essential Rumi. Translated by Coleman Barks. Penguin Books 1995.

choose how I react to them. Be angry by all means, because bad stuff happens to us, but accept things and move on. You can be upset because your partner has left you. However, it may well be that the relationship had run its course and you will now have the opportunity to meet the new person in your life; but you have to let go of the past.

I do believe that we are not given a challenge that we cannot deal with. The purpose of these things is to help us to learn and grow. Sometimes it takes time to appreciate the positive aspects of what happens to you!

There is a lovely book by Bernie Seigel[7] called 'Love, Medicine and Miracles'. It is a book about cancer and exceptional patients. A common theme from many of the patients was that they saw cancer as a gift that helped them to change their lives; to ditch the bad stuff and be themselves. Live their own lives and not the one that those around them gave them. It is a

---

[7] Bernie Seigel 1986 - Love, Medicine & Miracles - HarperCollins

marvellous and uplifting book. I actually think that this is a book about life, not illness.

Chapter fourteen

What to do?

- Do something different. If you do the same things in the same way you will inevitably end up with the same answer. Remember that you are here because you feel there is a need to change!
- Be you. Trust who you are. This is not a popularity contest. When you do different things or things differently accept that not everyone will be comfortable or supportive about this.
- Don't lose sight of reality, be grounded. Remember that bills will still need to be paid and that simply walking away from responsibilities may not be the best way forward. Do think of others!
- Listen to yourself, you know what gives you pleasure, what you love to do.
- Talk to people and listen – ask for help. Don't forget that by talking to people you will listen to yourself. You always know

more than you think. Give yourself credit for who you are.

- Be willing to explore – life is an adventure.
- If you try something and it doesn't work out, that's ok – try something else.
- We learn more when things do not go to plan.
- It's not about failing; it's about getting help to get it right!
- Ask for help when you sit quietly. You will be amazed at what seems to simply drop into your head, ideas, thoughts and realisations.

Life might seem easier when people tell us what we should or could do. However, nobody knows us like we do. It is important that we find and follow our own path. I do believe that it is the most worthwhile thing that we can do. Do not be seduced by those that tell you of a 5 or 6 step programme to success.

I do not want you to think that it is all about hard work with little reward. I do believe that the hard work is about starting the process.

When we begin to follow our path, things fall into place and become easier simply because we are being ourselves and that is actually very easy. We stop fighting ourselves. I wonder if what is challenging is the idea of change, rather than change itself?

Chapter fifteen

Thoughts for everyone

What if you don't believe in an afterlife? – Some thoughts on behaviour for non-spiritualists. (well, everybody really)

- Be kind to people – do things because it feels good, not because of what you might get back.
- Approach the world with positivity and optimism. Do not always assume the worst in people. The world is a wonderful place to explore.
- Trust your intuition/emotions on who and how you work with people, it will help to protect you from the nasty one's.
- Smile more, you will be amazed by the positive response it brings in others.
- Allow positive people into your life. It is truly astounding what can be achieved through positive attitudes.
- Clear out the negative people as they will only drag you down.

- Live in the now, carry the learning from the past and try not repeat the same mistakes.
- Love who you are. If you don't love yourself why expect others too?
- Take responsibility for what you do and who you are. Whilst your parents are responsible for you as a child and influence you, when you are over 21 it really is up to you. Don't be afraid to keep the good things your parents taught you and ditch the bad.
- Learn – it is normal to learn stuff for your job and to continue doing this throughout your working life. However, we are not generally taught to do the same with ourselves. It's no wonder that people have problems with relationships when they don't know what who they are and what they value. How can you share yourself if you don't know what it is that you want to share?
- Spend time on your personal development. It is so important to understand who you are, what you value, what you love. How

are you ever to find contentment if you are not following your dream, being true to yourself?

- Explore things. Be true to yourself. All of us are different to some extent, some people are naturally risk takers and some are not. I would not encourage you to do things that are way out of your comfort zone, stretch yourself by all means but understand that being a superhero is limited to a small number of people!
- Don't be envious of others, it is an unattractive trait. Contentment comes from being yourself, not by trying to be someone else.
- If you have a dream, turn it into reality by having a plan, otherwise that is all your dreams will ever be, dreams.
- Failure is part of learning. Getting things wrong is ok, it's how we learn. Getting things right all the time does not help us to learn and grow.

Ambition is good, it helps us to get better, to get on. There is nothing wrong in wanting to do better for yourself per se. Moving from a rented bedsit, to a flat, to a house, is positive. Working hard to get promotions at work to help provide for your family is fine. I believe that you need to put effort in to receive rewards. I have come across many people at work who do the minimum, behave cynically and complain about how they are always overlooked for promotion. I can't help but think, if this is the way they feel about their work, then they will often be the same about their life: Do the minimum and be negative about everything. And, by the way, it's never their fault!

I believe that you tend to get more out of things the more you put in.

Money matters. It is linked to ambition. There is nothing wrong with being materially wealthy. However, it is important that money becomes your servant and not your master. If it becomes your master, you are in danger of losing sight of what you are doing and why. You always have to ask the question; 'how is what I am doing adding real value to my life?' Yes, we need to have a reasonable level of income to ensure that we live with a level of comfort. But if you keep wanting more and more it might seem that there is nothing that will satisfy you. When is enough, enough? If you keep wanting more then there may be the danger that you are like an addict, never satisfied and always looking for the next hit. Having more and more money is not the answer. There was a joke told about Sigmund Freud who was asked whether he preferred to treat rich patients or poor patients. Freud replied that he always preferred to treat rich patients as they already knew that money was not the answer to their problems!

Money has no intrinsic value. It can be exchanged for things of value. When you stop exchanging it for food, holidays, treats and so forth and simply store it - not as part of your pension fund or just-in-case-money - does it really have any value, stuck in a bank? Is this really adding value to your life?

Having a big pile of money is obviously a measure or sign of success, rarely though is it a sign of contentment.

Give something back, help others and you will feel good. Whether you are coaching your child's football team, training guide puppies or helping at a charity shop, volunteering makes the world a better place. I do believe that if I give without the expectation of a return, I will feel better. It works.

I don't have to believe in God, or an afterlife to live a good life, to be fulfilled, to find contentment. You may possibly not use mediumship to help discover who you are so that you end up doing the things that truly suit you. There are lots of other ways to help you find out who the real 'you' is. I would encourage you to embrace who you are and to live your life fully and joyfully. How much better your life will be, not just for yourself but also for those around you. Not just your friends and family but for all those people that you will encounter on your journey.

Joy is something that is truly magical. Our lives can have moments of joy, to be savoured and enjoyed. I do feel that sometimes we have to open our eyes and open our hearts to know that it is there for us.

Life is wonderful and joyous, but maybe not all the time. I do believe that we were given all of our senses so that we could truly enjoy our lives here.

If I approach life as a child, I will see wondrous things and I will laugh at the absurd. There is much we can learn from children. Be childlike, not childish.

Please choose what you do.

The importance of thank you

This may seem obvious – however it is often forgotten – saying thank you to people for the things they do for you makes a big difference to the people you say it to. It is about not taking people for granted. It is about recognising what people do, you are giving them your attention.

The worst thing you can do to anyone is to ignore them.

Chapter sixteen

Some final thoughts

There is very little that is new. Very little that has not been said before and, probably, better. However, it will all be new to me. That's the point.

We come here to learn and experience new things. Our parents, wanting to care and help us, will often tell us what to do and what to avoid in order to protect us. But we do need to experience all that life has to offer.

Words cannot always convey the meaning of certain things. I can talk about love and how magical it is and, if I were a poet, I might be able to convey some aspects of love. However, words cannot express clearly the feelings connected to love; when your heart races at the thought of the person and you get that strange feeling in the pit of your stomach. You feel both excited and scared at the same time. I can talk about love, but you need to experience love to really begin to understand what it means.

You have to experience life for it to become real for you. Other people, in their desire to help you learn, can tell you things but you need to experience things for yourself in order for them to be real. I cannot live my life through the experiences of others. Sometimes, there are no shortcuts.

Sometimes we learn our lessons the hard way. I do believe that we only learn when we are ready.

I also believe that we are destined to repeat our mistakes until we are ready to learn from them. I was in my twenties working for a travel company and had a challenging piece of work to complete. I felt that I had to do this on my own and that to ask for help was a clear sign of weakness. I ended up working all the hours to try to finish the task and I was run ragged. As a consequence of not asking for help I almost lost my job. It wasn't until my late forties working in a new job when I was struggling again that it eventually dawned on me to ask for help. The main thing I learned was that people wanted to help but they needed to be asked first. I finished the task that was set, and I learnt so much from the people around me. It had only taken me twenty plus years to learn my lesson! I do try now not to repeat this mistake. I wasn't ready in my twenties. By the way, as my friends would tell you, I am still making mistakes, still learning. Learning is lifelong.

It also took me a long time to learn that you cannot help others unless they are ready. When I stopped work in my fifties and did some voluntary numeracy teaching, I came across a number of people who were bright and capable and had made the difficult decision to accept their limitations with regard to numeracy. Yet they failed to attend classes to help their development. I realised that people will only make the changes necessary when they are ready, not when you think they are. You have to leave people alone, and allow them to be themselves, to be willing to offer help but to be ok when people choose not to take up the offer.

I have more than enough to worry about in my own life than to worry about everyone else.

There is a lovely quote from the Gospel of Thomas[8]: Logion 26:

> *'You detect a speck in your brother's eye but fail to perceive the beam sticking out from your own. Remove the timber from your own eye, and you will see clearly enough to extract the speck lodged in the eye of your brother.'*

Sort yourself out first before you worry about others!

Wisdom is not just about knowledge; it is about knowing how to use it.

To come back to the theme that there is very little that is new I want to quote from Marcus Aurelius[9] and his book, Meditations:

> *'… then what is to be prized… I think it is this: to do (and not to do) what we were designed for. That's the goal of all trades,*

---

[8] The Gospel of Thomas. Translated by Lynn Bauman. White Cloud Press 2003.

[9] Marcus Aurelius. Meditations. Translated by Gregory Hays 2003. Weidenfeld and Nicolson.

all arts, and what each of them aims at: that the thing they create should do what it was designed to do. The nurseryman who cares for the vines, the horse trainer, the dog breeder- this is what they aim at. And teaching and education – what else are they trying to accomplish?

So that's what you should prize. Hold onto that, and you won't be tempted to aim at anything else.

And what if you can't stop prizing a lot of other things? Then you'll never be free - free, independent, imperturbable. Because you'll always be envious and jealous, afraid that people might come and take it all away from you.' Book 6.

So, this is the challenge, to be yourself. To spend time understanding who you are. To live your life in harmony with who you are, not what other people may want you to be. To find contentment. To live a life that is full of love and joy and enables you to deal with all the challenges that it throws up. To know that you have within you all the tools that will guide you. Not just in what you do, but also how you do it.

For me the key to understanding who I am comes from my mediumship, trusting my emotions, my feelings and being guided by them. This is simply my way. There are others.

Whatever you believe about what happens after we die; I do think that we feel better knowing that we have made the most of our lives. Feelings of resentment and anger are clear signs that we are not at peace, not content. Lives full of comparisons are always doomed to failure because it is not about what others do, it is about what we do.

Please remember that it is never too late to make the changes you want to in the way you live your life.

Chapter seventeen

Winning the Lottery

About 10 years ago I was travelling back from a cycling trip in the French Alps with my good friend, Mark. As was usual on such long drives, topics for conversation were quite wide ranging and we started talking about winning the lottery. I asked Mark what he would do if he won. He replied, nothing. I asked why. He said that he had no need to change anything as he had a job he loved, both as a General Practitioner and as a research scientist. He was also able to enjoy the outdoors, whether it was walking, cycling or mountaineering. He said that in a way he had already won the lottery.

Mark's view of the world has stayed with me.

A couple of years ago I was out for a cycle and thinking about my upcoming talk at a Spiritualist church. That conversation with Mark about the lottery came to mind. As I mulled over this chat, it dawned on me that, through my involvement with Spiritualism, I too had won the lottery.

Chapter eighteen

Further Reading

The Language of Emotions – Karla McLaren. Sounds True. ISBN 978-1-59179-769-2

A Guide to Spirit Healing – Harry Edwards

Compendium and Digest of the Works of Andrew Jackson-Davis. ISBN 978-1-291-54475-6

Elisabeth Kubler-Ross. Life Lessons. ISBN 978-0-7432-0811-6

Elisabeth Kubler-Ross. The Wheel of Life. ISBN 0-553-50544-0

Martin Seligman. Flourish – A new Understanding of Happiness and Well-Being. ISBN 978-1-85788-569-9

Hare Brain, Tortoise Brain. Why Intelligence Increases when you think Less. Guy Claxton. ISBN 1-85702-709-4

The Tao of Pooh. Benjamin Hoff. ISBN 0-416-19511-3

Winnie the Pooh. A.A.Milne

The Lakota Way. Stories and Lessons for Living. Joseph M. Marshall 111. ISBN 978-0-14-219609-0

You Can Heal Your Life. Louise Hay. ISBN 0-937611-01-8

The Art of War. Sun Tzu. ISBN 1-57062-904-8

Grief Works. Julia Samuel. ISBN 978-0-241-27077-6

Indian Spirit. Edited by Michael Oren Fitzgerald & Judith Fitzgerald. ISBN 978-1-9333316-19-2

The Power of Now. Eckhart Tolle. ISBN 978-0-340-73350-9

Emotional Intelligence. Daniel Goleman. ISBN 978-0747528302

The Examined Life – How we Find and Lose Ourselves. Stephen Grosz. ISBN 978-0-099-54903-1

Best of Both Worlds. A Tribute to a great Medium. Rosalind Cattanach. ISBN 0953481603

Chapter nineteen

Teachings of the Cowichan Tribe

I came across these teachings when I was in Canada; Duncan, Vancouver Island to be precise. I was very fortunate to spend time with tribal elders who taught me a great deal about how they aspire to live. When you read them, I feel sure, that, like me, you will see how spiritual and practical they are.

Initially, I wasn't sure whether to share these teachings. However, it feels right to do so….

SNUW'UY'ULH

THE COWICHAN TEACHINGS

The Family is the heart of life

Honour the elders

Each person is important

Everything in nature is part of our family – we are all relatives

Live in harmony with nature

Take care of the earth and take only what you need

Take care of your health

Be positive

Enjoy today

Share what you have

Be honest and truthful in all that you do and say

Do the best you can do, be the best you can be

Learn from one another

Respect the rights of others

Respect your leaders and their decisions

Chapter twenty

Some Questions to ask Yourself

Do I feel content with my life? Remember the contentment is not about perfection or the absence of problems but rather a sense of being at peace with yourself.

What is it about my life that makes me feel discontent?

Am I able to express clearly what is wrong?

If I can't articulate what is making me discontent, who can help me? Friends? Coach? Family? Teacher?

How is my life divided up? Ie Work, friends, family, me time?

How do I feel about these parts of my life?

Which aspects of my life do I want to change and why?

What changes do I feel I want to make?

What do I need to actually do to make the changes?

How long will it take to make the changes?

Am I ready to make changes?

What resources do I need to make things happen?

Who have I talked to about these changes?

Who are the people I can trust and confide in?

Who will help me to make these changes?

After you make your changes what do I want my life to feel like, look like and be like?

What may be the consequences of making changes in my life on me, my friends, my family?

How will I manage these consequences?

How will I set realistic goals for any changes I want to make?

How will I celebrate when I make the changes I want?

To protect privacy some names have been changed.

Printed in Poland
by Amazon Fulfillment
Poland Sp. z o.o., Wrocław

56505168R00073